Contents

Studying arctic life

△ *The Eskimos lived almost entirely off the animals they hunted, eating the meat and using the hides to make clothing and homes. This woman is chewing a piece of sealskin, which makes it softer and easier to work with.*

All human beings need food and shelter to survive. Many also have a system of beliefs that gives shape and meaning to their lives. Throughout history, people have created different ways of meeting these basic requirements. By studying the peoples of the **Arctic** and **subarctic** we learn how they used the resources around them to build shelters and find food, and how they developed a way of life that sustained them.

IN THIS BOOK we will look at how arctic peoples lived about 200 years ago, before their lives were changed by the arrival of Europeans and Americans. We can build up a picture of the Eskimo way of life from the stories told by present-day arctic peoples, writings of early explorers and traders, and the studies of **anthropologists** and **archaeologists**. In this way we can begin to understand Eskimo culture.

◁ *Eskimos fished and hunted land and sea mammals in all weather conditions.*

MAKE it WORK!

ARCTIC
PEOPLES

Andrew Haslam & Alexandra Parsons

TWO-CAN
in association with
WATTS BOOKS

First published in Great Britain in 1995 by
Two-Can Publishing Ltd
346 Old Street
London EC1V 9NQ
in association with
Watts Books
96 Leonard Street
London EC2A 4RH

A catalogue record for this book is available from the British Library.

Hardback ISBN: 1 85434 274 6
Paperback ISBN: 1 85434 275 4

Managing Editor: Christine Morley
Editor: Jacqueline McCann
Designer: Helen McDonagh
Art Director: Jill Plank
Deputy Art Director: Carole Orbell
Picture Researcher: Sam Riley
Model-makers: Paul Holzherr, Melanie Williams

Thanks also to: Colin and Jenny at Plough Studios.

Models: Anton Ajetunmobi, Daniel Bradford, Vanisha Cozier, Tendai Dhliwayo, James Hensby, Zakiyyah Hussain,
Emily McClymont, Michael Manatsa, CJ Marshall, Lynette Marshall, Thomas O'Brian, Emma Sainsbury, Anna Smith

Photographic credits:
Arthur Phillips: p9, p59 (maps); Bryan & Cherry Alexander: p5 (tl, br), p 12 (tr), p20, p29, p36, p37, p40, p42, p44, p46, p48 (bl),
p60 (ml, br), p61; British Museum: p30, p34 (tr), p60 (tr); Canadian Museum of Civilization: p4 (no. 39638), p32 (bl, no. 51166);
Derek Fordham: p5 (bl); Magnum: F Mayer, p23, p32 (tl); McCord Museum of Canadian History, Notman Photographic Archives:
p28 (no. MP595(2)), p38, (no. MP1971(9)), p48 (tr, no. MP597(186)); National Archives of Canada: p31 (no. PA110844), p47
(no. PA114667); Range/Bettmann: p45, p50, p58 (2); Werner Forman Archive: p12 (br), p35, p56.

All other photographs by Jon Barnes
Printed and bound by G. Canale & C. SpA, Turin, Italy

Hardback 2 4 6 8 10 9 7 5 3 1
Paperback 2 4 6 8 10 9 7 5 3 1

THE ARCTIC is the most northerly region of the world. It is a vast wilderness of mountains, **tundra** and ice. The subarctic is the area directly south of the Arctic Circle, below the **tree line**. Despite the enormous size of the Arctic and subarctic, the peoples who lived and continue to live there found similar solutions to the problems they faced. We have used the following divisions, where necessary, to introduce information that relates more to one group than another (see page 7).

KEY FOR SYMBOLS

🏠 (snowhouse) **eastern Arctic**

🐋 (bowhead whale) **western Arctic**

🎾 (snow-shoe) **subarctic**

THE STORY OF ARCTIC SETTLEMENT is really the story of how people developed the skills necessary to exploit a very cold and inhospitable climate. The Arctic is rich in terms of food resources, but the demands of day-to-day life were such that people had to be extremely tough, both physically and mentally, to survive.

COMMON TO ALL PEOPLES OF THE ARCTIC was the belief that the world around them and all things in it had both a practical and sacred aspect. Their world was dominated by many spirits. Everything, from mountains to stones or **artefacts**, was believed to possess a spirit, just as animals and people did. It is important to remember that everything in the Eskimo's world had a deep religious significance.

THE WORD 'ESKIMO' has been used for many years by Europeans and Americans to refer to arctic peoples, although it is not an arctic word. It is thought to be an Ojibwa Indian word meaning 'raw meat eaters', or a Montagnais word meaning 'snow-shoes'. In general, arctic peoples such as **Inuits** and **Yupiks**, referred themselves with words that mean 'real human beings'. However, as there is no single word that covers all the different groups of people living in the Arctic and subarctic, we shall use Eskimo.

◁ *The winter camp of Siberian caribou herders.*

THE MAKE IT WORK! way of looking at history is to ask questions of the past and find some of the answers by making replicas of the things people made. However, you do not have to make everything in the book to understand the arctic peoples' way of life. Some of the objects included are based on sacred or ceremonial traditions and therefore should be treated with respect.

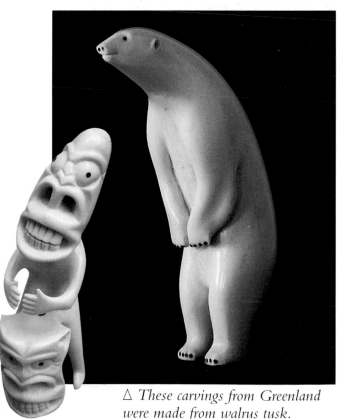

△ *These carvings from Greenland were made from walrus tusk.*

A harsh, icy haven

Thousands of years ago, during the **Ice Age**, the ice cap at the top of the world was a great deal larger than it is today. The climate was also considerably colder and the sea level much lower. What are now shallow seas were then dry land, and Siberia, Alaska, northern Canada, the Aleutian islands and Greenland were all linked together.

▷ *This is a relief map of the arctic region.*

BIG GAME HUNTERS headed northwards during the Ice Age. They came in large groups from the empty plains of northern Asia and Siberia, following herds of mammoth and other animals. They crossed the Bering Sea land bridge and spread outwards from Alaska to as far away as Greenland. Later, the ice cap melted and sea covered the land between Siberia and Alaska, making it difficult to return.

IN THE NORTH the hunters found an icy wilderness, where the soil could not be cultivated and few trees grew. But they also found plentiful supplies of fresh water and abundant wildlife: whales, walrus, seals, **caribou** (known as reindeer in Europe), birds and musk ox. Over many centuries, people adapted to a life of snow, ice and chilling winds.

▽ *Indigenous vegetation.*

moss

berries

fir tree
(tree line)

▷ *Indigenous wildlife.*

polar bear

caribou

wolf

reindeer

arctic fox

walrus

seal

whale

salmon

arctic char

ptarmigan

guillemot

nesting birds

THE EASTERN ARCTIC refers to the polar regions of Greenland and eastern Canada.

Eastern Arctic peoples:

Greenland: *Inuit*
E. Canada: *Inuit, Netsilik*

THE WESTERN ARCTIC refers to the polar regions of North America, western Canada and the Aleutian Islands.

Western Arctic peoples:

Western Canada: *Copper Inuit*
Aleutian Islands: ***Aleut***
Alaska: *Inuit, Yupik*

THE SUBARCTIC is the area south of the Arctic Circle. It covers the north of the American continent, the top of the Asian landmass and the most northerly areas of Europe.

Subarctic peoples:

N. American Indians: *Cree, Kutchin*
Eurasians: *Chukchi, Yakuty, Nentsy Eveny, Evenki*
Europeans: *Saami (Lapps)*

The arctic climate

The Arctic is actually a desert made up almost completely of ice. As it hardly ever rains, there is very little snow. Temperatures are well below zero for most of the year, and freezing winds whip across the landscape. However, during the short summer, the sun shines for much of the day and the ice melts to reveal scrubland.

SPRING in the Arctic usually begins during March. It is still cold, but the days are getting longer and the sun begins to shine. Seals come out of the sea to bask in the sun, so the Eskimos would move on to the ice to hunt the seals, before the ice became too thin to walk on. As the temperature rises, the ice begins to thaw and break up and the hunters leave the ice floe to live on the land.

▽ *The Arctic in summer: temperatures rise and the ice recedes. Eskimos move to new hunting grounds.*

portable summer dwelling

permafrost stops trees and shrubs taking root

hunters move to the tundra in summer

THE SUN SHINES for at least part of the day from March to September and temperatures in some inland regions can rise to 16° centigrade. The sun melts the ice and snow covering the land, but it does not reach the **permafrost**, a permanently frozen layer of soil under the surface.

DURING SUMMER, mosses, grasses, lichens and low shrubs grow on the vast swampy plain, or tundra, that extends from the polar ice cap in the north, to the tree line in the south. The Eskimos would travel inland to hunt the huge caribou herds that came to graze on the tundra.

▷ *Men travel to the edge of the **ice floe**. They hunt for seals and fish for tom-cod and char through **breathing holes**.*

hunters build temporary homes

A WHITEOUT is a deadly arctic hazard. It happens mainly on cloudy summer days when light seems to come from all around, casting no shadows. It is impossible to tell left from right, or north from south. The only thing to do is sit still and wait for the light to change.

▽ *In summer the earth tilts towards the sun.*

Sun ▽

▽ *In winter the earth tilts away from the sun.*

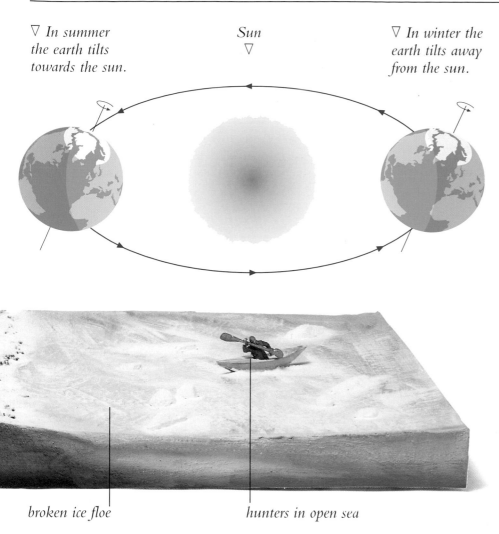

◁ *The earth spins around the sun, turning on its own axis. In the first half of the year the earth tilts towards the sun; in the second half it tilts away – this is why we have seasons.*

ARCTIC SEASONS are very distinct from one another. In summer, the sun rarely sinks below the horizon and there is almost continual daylight. In winter, the sun's rays are at such a low angle that they hardly rise above the horizon. It is almost permanently dark.

◁ *In late spring and summer Eskimos hunt in coastal areas from their **kayaks**.*

BY EARLY WINTER, the ice has frozen to around three metres deep and is safe to walk on. The lack of daylight makes hunting difficult, but it is possible to fish through holes cut in the ice. Eskimos also hunted in areas of open sea, called **polynyas**, which never freeze over due to strong currents.

broken ice floe   *hunters in open sea*

IN AUTUMN, temperatures begin to fall and the caribou start to migrate south. When **freeze-up** begins, the sea ices over, preventing boat travel. While the ice is soft, it is also dangerous walk on. During this time, the Eskimos would hunt the last of the caribou and perhaps dig a new **sod house**.

▽ *The Arctic in winter – temperatures drop and Eskimos move on to the ice to hunt sea mammals.*

huskies pulling sleds

Keeping warm – staying alive

Keeping warm was a matter of life and death in the Arctic, and clothes were the Eskimo's main defence against the cold. Animal skins were sewn together very carefully with animal **sinews** to make warm clothing. Arctic peoples had very distinctive ways of decorating their clothes, using feathers, bones, or bird quills, not only as decorations, but also as **amulets**. Above all, they thanked the spirit of the animal that clothed them.

EACH GROUP OF PEOPLE developed its own characteristic look which was reflected in its costumes. This meant that strangers approaching a settlement could be recognized from a safe distance simply by their outline.

PEOPLE OF THE SUBARCTIC were spread out over a wide area. In Siberia and other parts of Eurasia, caribou skins were often used to make clothes, while North American Indians also used moose hides. Common to all groups was the use of the snow-shoe. In winter, these tennis-racquet-shaped, strap-on soles made it easier to cross drifts of soft snow without sinking.

snow-shoes

caribou-skin tunic

harpoon

caribou-skin tunic

loose, all-in-one caribou suits worn by mother and baby

subarctic Indian hunter

Chukchi woman from Siberia

Inuit hunter from Canadian eastern Arct

WESTERN ARCTIC MEN, such as the Yupik, wore **labrets** – decorated plugs of ivory or bone, pushed into holes cut on either side of the mouth. These holes were cut during a boy's teenage years. He was expected to show no signs of pain during the ceremony. A man with labrets was seen to be ready for hunting, responsibility and marriage.

WESTERN ARCTIC WOMEN took advantage of Alaska's rich supply of fur-bearing animals, such as ground squirrel, wolf and mink, to make highly decorated costumes. They wore jewellery in the form of earrings and strings of beads, and were tattooed in their teens (see page 53).

EASTERN ARCTIC PEOPLES depended on large sea mammals such as the seal, walrus and whale. By necessity their clothing had to be waterproof as they spent so much time hunting on the ice. In the polar regions, warm leg coverings made from polar bear skins were worn.

WATERPROOF CLOTHING was needed for fishing trips. It was either made of sealskin or strips of sea mammal intestine sewn tightly together. Bird skin clothing was also light, waterproof, durable and warm. These were important alternatives for clothing in the eastern Arctic, where caribou were not common.

finger masks

plain, loose-fitting parka

long caribou-skin parka with rounded flap at front

Inuit woman from Alaska

eastern Arctic, Iglulik **shaman**

eastern Arctic child

ARCTIC PEOPLES were always on the move, from summer camps to winter camps, hunting animals. As a result, their homes had to be either light and portable, or fast to build, using materials that were readily available. During the winter, some Eskimos lived in sod houses. Dug deep beneath the earth for warmth and insulation, they were like huge underground caves. A sod house could also be reused the following winter, if it had not been too badly damaged during the year. Although an ideal winter home, the sod house was too damp and warm for summer.

MEN STARTED WORK ON THE SOD HOUSE when the surface soil had thawed. A wide hole, one or two metres in depth, was dug into the earth to form a communal living area. The entrance was very small, so that the heat from inside could not escape. Some houses were built for one family, while others were up to 20 metres long and home to extended families. At the top of the sod house the air was warmer, so people slept on raised platforms. In some of the larger houses, these were shared by up to 50 people.

MAKE A SOD HOUSE

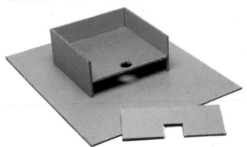

You will need: wooden fruit box, cardboard, short twigs, scraps of sacking, moss (from a florist), glue, craft knife, cutting mat, scraps of fur fabric

1 Cut the base, four walls (one with a door) and floor (with a round hole) as shown above left. Glue together. Cut and glue the side of the entrance tunnel and the outer walls into place.

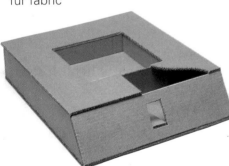

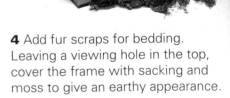

2 Cut and fit sections to cover the ground level. Cut entrance door on 3 sides and fold along bottom to form tunnel. Cut out section to view.

3 Ask an adult to cut wood strips from the fruit box. Glue these to the walls and floor. Build roof frame and sleeping platform with sticks.

4 Add fur scraps for bedding. Leaving a viewing hole in the top, cover the frame with sacking and moss to give an earthy appearance.

IN PARTS OF NORTHERN ALASKA, people lived in permanent whaling communities. Sod houses were lived in all year round. The houses and their occupants were given names such as 'The people with lots of mice', or 'All wet around it', and 'The people who face the sun'.

SEAL-OIL LAMPS usually belonged to the wife in a family group. In the evening, a woman would light the moss wick and place her lamp on the raised platform. The heat that was generated by the slow-burning lamp and the body heat of the people inside, kept everyone warm.

a gap in the roof lets in light (sometimes transparent sea-mammal intestine is used as a window pane)

THE ENTRANCE TO A SOD HOUSE was via an underground passage that also served as a storage and cooking area. Before entering the sod house, an Eskimo would use an *anautaq*, or snow-beater, to brush the snow off his or her outer garments. Then he would take off his mittens, boots and parka and hang them up to dry over a seal-oil lamp.

single platform for sleeping on

framework of whalebone or wood, covered with sods of earth and sealskin

chambers for storing food and drying clothes

△ *Many Siberian peoples, such as the Eveny, Chukchi and Koryak, kept herds of caribou. The caribou provided their herders with milk, meat and hides, and could also be ridden.*

🐋 🛖 **CARIBOU** are wild North American reindeer. They spend the summer on the tundra and go south for the winter to the forests below the tree line. Hunters did not chase after caribou, as it was too exhausting for them to run in their heavy clothes. Instead, they would lay an ambush. In order to work out which route the caribou would take, the hunters studied the weather and used their knowledge of how the herds had behaved in the past. If that failed, they would consult a shaman.

▽ *These Copper Inuit men use distinctive curved bows and arrows made from wood and sinew. As caribou are curious and short-sighted animals, the hunters were able to get very close before shooting with deadly accuracy.*

WHEN SETTING AN AMBUSH, hunters knew that the caribou preferred to cross rivers and lakes at narrow, shallow points. They built corrals, or enclosures, in a huge V shape at the water's edge to drive the animals to one spot, where they were speared with lances by men in kayaks. To capture caribou on land, the animals were driven into a circular corral of poles where they would be trapped with snares, or fall into pits. Bows and arrows were used to pick off individual animals that were too widely spread out to be ambushed.

WATCHING FOR HERDS OF GAME required endless patience and warm clothing. The hunter sat motionless, scanning the horizon for the slightest movement. For the Eskimos, the landscape was alive; they believed that every rock and fold of land had a spirit that, if in a good mood, would help the hunter.

a hunter waits in the shallows to spear caribou

POLAR BEARS were highly prized arctic mammals. They were hunted in the late spring, when the mother bear was holed up in her den with her pups. Killing a polar bear required great skill and was cause for celebration. Their hides were very useful, but polar-bear meat, unless well cooked, was poisonous.

a caribou crosses at a narrow point in the river

a kayak moves swiftly through shallow waters

women and children scare the caribou

stone mounds, or cairns, built in the shape of humans help to divert the caribou

some caribou trapped in corrals

The arctic diet

There were very few vegetables or fruits, no grains to make bread and no starchy food such as potatoes. The Eskimo diet consisted almost entirely of meat and fish. They kept healthy by eating every part of the animal. They ate the fat, eyes, organs, stomach contents and blood to give them all the minerals, vitamins and fibre they needed on this high-protein diet. For variety, they matured pieces of meat for a stronger flavour – just as we eat strong blue cheese. Matured seal–flipper was much prized as a tasty morsel.

▷ *This Nentsy girl is cooking over an open fire. When wood was available, food was often grilled and roasted.*

BANNOCK is a type of bread which was introduced to the Eskimos by Scottish whalers. The original recipe used water, but in the recipe below we have used yoghurt for more flavour.

MAKE BANNOCK BREAD

You will need: 450 g plain flour, 1 tsp salt, 1 tsp bicarbonate of soda, 300 ml plain yoghurt or buttermilk, a large frying pan with a lid, oil for cooking

1 Sift together the flour, salt and bicarbonate of soda in a large bowl.

2 Add the yoghurt or buttermilk to the flour mixture and mix into a soft dough, adding water if necessary.

3 Turn out the dough on to a floured board and knead for 5 minutes. Form into rolls. Ask an adult to oil the pan and place it over a medium heat.

4 Add rolls to the pan, cover and reduce the heat. After 3 minutes, turn the rolls over, replace the lid and cook for another 3 minutes until the rolls are golden brown. Leave to cool.

FRESH WATER was obtained from melted ice, or from snow. Eskimos preferred to melt ice, because snow, which is made up almost entirely of air, takes a long time to melt and large quantities are needed just to make a little water.

FOOD WAS COOKED in a cauldron suspended over a seal-oil lamp or, in regions where wood was available, over an open fire. A hunk of meat or fish was usually boiled in water, and the remaining liquid made a nutritious soup.

IN SUMMER, in parts of the southern Arctic, berries, edible leaves and roots added variety to the Eskimo's basic diet of meat and fish. Seaweed was also eaten in parts of southern Alaska.

FOOD WAS PRESERVED by drying it in the sun and air, or by freezing. Drying could only be done during the warm summer months. Meat was cut into strips and left outside for a couple of days, then packed into bags of seal blubber. Meat or fish prepared in this way lasted almost a year. Frozen meat did not last as long as dried, and a lamp was needed to defrost it. If lamps were not available, frozen meat was chewed. Food was often stored in the ice until required.

▽ *Bannock became a staple food for the Eskimos, making them dependent on supplies of flour brought in by European and American traders.*

SEA MAMMAL FAT was used for all sorts of things. Chunks of it made an enjoyable snack. If it was left and kept away from sunlight it turned into clear liquid. This was used to light and heat Eskimo homes, and was used as a medicine, a skin cream and insect repellent in the summer.

FISH AND SHELLFISH were a vital source of food, as were waterfowl and birds which nested on the cliff edges. The most important types of fish, such as salmon and char, are migratory, and therefore only available for a short season.

MEAL TIMES were not fixed; people ate when they were hungry. Food was laid out on the floor and the hunter made the first cut. After that, everyone helped themselves, using their own knives to cut off portions of meat.

Arts and crafts of the Arctic

For most of the year, Eskimos had little time to devote to purely decorative crafts. However, during the two to three months of continuous darkness in winter, men and women spent many hours perfecting their skills in making clothes, weapons and artefacts. Practically every man and woman was in some sense an artist, and well-crafted objects were much admired. Eskimos saw no difference between making things that were useful, beautiful, or religious. Instead, all these qualities were combined when making even the most ordinary of things, from a hairpin to a fish hook or clothes basket.

△ *These Aleut baskets, on sale at a trading post, were made by hand. They were woven from dune grass, gathered on the coast during the summer months.*

JEWELLERY, such as earrings, necklaces and belts, was often made with a base of softened sealskin. Animal teeth and walrus ivory were used to decorate the skin, along with feathers, birds' claws and bills. Ivory or bone beads were also used and, later, glass **tradebeads** became popular.

SUBARCTIC SIBERIANS, such as the Koryak, made bracelets, earrings and pendants from iron, brass and copper. The Eveny people wore brass pendants called 'throat medals' tied around their necks with leather thongs. The pendants were believed to protect the wearer from colds.

MAKE A BASKET

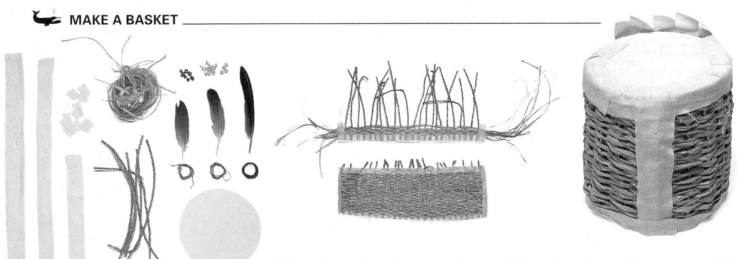

You will need: twine cut into 25 cm lengths, raffia, masking tape, needle and different coloured thread, card, calico strips 3 cm wide x 40 cm long, small calico squares, paint, glue, beads, feathers, scissors

1 Cut a piece of masking tape about 40 cm long. Stick down lengths of twine about 1.5 cm apart. Tape this row of twine to your work surface.

2 Now weave raffia in and out of the twine until you have a woven piece measuring about 25 cm x 40 cm.

3 Tape the edges of the weaving with masking tape. Then bend the weaving around to form a tube. Place the tube on card, draw a circle to fit the base. Cut this out and tape over the base.

4 Glue calico strips around the joins at the base, the rim and the seam.

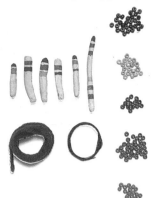

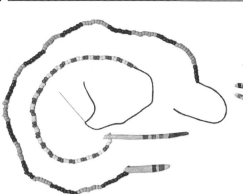

You will need: small glass beads, coloured thread, paint, thick wool, self-hardening clay, needle

1 Make 8 long thin beads out of the clay. Make a hole in the top of each one and leave to dry. Paint as above.

2 Thread 4 strands of beads, making patterns with the colours as above. Tie the long beads on to the ends.

3 Tie up the strands with two lengths of wool. Tie the wool lengths to form a loop and hook over each ear.

5 For a necklace, make clay fish shapes as shown right. Paint, then thread with beads on to 2 pieces of string tied together.

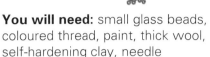 **ALEUT BASKET MAKERS** also used one of the most unusual of all basket-weaving materials – fibres from the baleen of the bowhead whale, a type of whale that lives by filtering plankton out of seawater. Baleen baskets had ivory lid handles carved in the shape of a seal or whale's tail. They were popular items for trade.

THE PACIFIC ALEUTS of southwest Alaska, made baskets that were mainly used for carrying fish. The grasses were split with the fingernails into strands as thin as silk threads. Some strands were dyed to weave patterns into the baskets.

▷ *Baskets like these were used for storing precious household possessions and clothes.*

5 Paint the small calico squares with bright colours as shown. Then glue them on to the basket. Thread the string with several coloured beads and sew these on. Decorate the seams with patterns made from coloured threads, and stitch some feathers around the top.

Between two worlds

Today, Eskimos have many of the conveniences of modern day life. They live in permanent homes with central heating and watch television. They use snowmobiles (skidoos) instead of sleds and dogs and regular air services connect them to the rest of the world. However, aspects of their lives are still very traditional. Living off the land is still very important and crafts such as sewing skins, carving and basket-making still thrive.

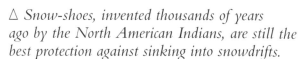

△ *Snow-shoes, invented thousands of years ago by the North American Indians, are still the best protection against sinking into snowdrifts.*

A SNOWMOBILE is a motorised version of the traditional sled. It is now the fastest way of travelling across the Arctic. A snowmobile owner needs to be an excellent mechanic: if his machine breaks down far from home, he could die unless he is able to repair it quickly. Arctic peoples rarely keep husky dogs now, except for tracking seal breathing holes, or for racing in dog-sled events.

KAYAKS are rarely seen in the Arctic today. However, they are now used in all parts of the world, mainly for sport and recreation.

△ *This Saami caribou herder takes a break during the spring move to summer pastures in northern Norway. Snowmobiles are very fast, reducing journey times from days to hours.*

THE ESKIMOS DESIGNED specialist equipment for the arctic environment that has never really been bettered. Their boats, clothes, tools and weapons form the basis of the most sophisticated cold-weather gear used by people in northern regions of the world today.

HARPOONS are still used to hunt sea mammals. These weapons have the same basic mechanism of a throwing stick with a detachable point, just as they had thousands of years ago. Modern skis have also remained true to their original design – long and slender with curved tips – which was based on wood or whalebone sled runners.

▷ *The work of Inuit soapstone carvers is very highly skilled and is in great demand from collectors, museums and art galleries. Both men and women carve, and by selling their art they can supplement their income. This man from Qeqertat in Greenland is carving out a figure from local stone.*

◁ *The parka is an original Eskimo design that is still the best way to keep warm in freezing weather.*

THE ART OF THE ARCTIC is alive and well. A whole new generation of modern artists is producing sculptures, baskets, drawings and prints in the traditional way. Some of the artefacts are sold to tourists, while other items are bought by collectors for very high prices, enabling small communities to earn a reasonable living.

FESTIVALS AND GAMES are keeping the stories, dances, songs and skills of the Arctic alive. Blanket toss, seal skinning and touchball are some of the activities that are still practised today.

IN THE PAST FORTY YEARS, the Eskimos have endured a complete upheaval in the way of life that served them so well for 3,000 years. However, such is the strength of their culture that many traditions have survived and are being rediscovered and taken up by today's generation.

THE PARKA is so successful a design that it has been copied around the world. Modern parkas are less bulky because of the use of man-made fabrics and fillings, but it is doubtful that they are as warm as the original garment. Today, although Eskimos wear shop-bought clothes, such as jeans and T-shirts, they still wrap up in sealskin or caribou trousers and a fur-trimmed parka in the winter or when hunting on the ice. Skins are still prepared in the traditional way by women.

HUNTERS are still greatly respected among arctic peoples – even though some of them now have jobs and can only hunt at the weekend. School holidays are timed to coincide with spring hunting or summer fishing, so the children can go camping with their parents and learn how to hunt in the traditional way.

▷ *This Inuit father and son wait patiently by a breathing hole in late spring. It is important to the Inuit that their children learn how to hunt and fish.*

Index